BUS COMPANY
SERVICE VEHICLES

MALCOLM BATTEN

AMBERLEY

First published 2021

Amberley Publishing
The Hill, Stroud
Gloucestershire, GL5 4EP

www.amberley-books.com

Copyright © Malcolm Batten, 2021

The right of Malcolm Batten to be identified
as the Author of this work has been asserted in
accordance with the Copyrights, Designs and
Patents Act 1988.

ISBN 978 1 3981 0474 7 (print)
ISBN 978 1 3981 0475 4 (ebook)

British Library Cataloguing in Publication Data.
A catalogue record for this book is available from
the British Library.

Orgination by Amberley Publishing.
Printed in the UK.

Introduction

In the days before deregulation and privatisation, many companies adapted old buses for a variety of specialist uses as service vehicles. Using the skills and ingenuity of their workshops, buses might variously become stores vans, uniform stores etc. Buses were also eminently suited for conversion to information vehicles, able to promote a range of services such as new ticketing schemes, route changes, holiday tours and private hire facilities. These might be sited in a bus station or city centre but could also travel to outdoor events like town shows and promote the company's wares.

Accidents and breakdowns will happen in even the best-maintained fleets so a towing vehicle would be needed equipped with a towing bar, or a recovery vehicle with a crane and equipment for raising a bus that had toppled on its side. Some bus operators converted old buses as towing lorries to rescue broken-down vehicles. Others preferred ex-military trucks such as the AEC Matador. First introduced in 1939, some 9,000 of these four-wheel drive 'medium artillery tractors' were built for the War Department and were readily snapped up when they became surplus. These came with somewhat austere cabs, but here again the bodyshop would often come up with a custom-built body using various bus parts. There would be accommodation for the recovery crew and space for their equipment. In later years, more modern former commercial vehicles might be acquired and adapted for a towing/recovery role. Towing vehicles often ran on trade plates, with the original registration removed, making identification more difficult.

Trams remained in some municipal fleets in the 1950s. Glasgow was the last fleet to dispense with these in 1962, leaving only Blackpool until the revival led by Manchester in the 1990s. Trolleybuses were still also in use in a number of mainly municipal fleets through the 1950s and 1960s, but after London Transport chose to eliminate them from its fleet, finally removing them in 1962, the manufacture of new trolleybuses for a limited market became uneconomic and the remaining companies withdrew theirs. Bradford had been one of the first two trolleybus operators starting out in June 1911, and as one of the staunchest supporters of the 'silent servants' they were the last to dispense with them on 23 March 1972. These trolleybus operators needed tower wagons to maintain the overhead wires (just as tram operators had before them). These could be either purpose-built or, again, converted from buses in their fleets. In the early days of tram operation, preceding motor vehicles, manual or horse-drawn tower wagons had been in use.

Overhanging trees can cause havoc to the roofs and windows of double-deck buses. In former days some companies used to have a tree-lopping vehicle to prune offending branches. This would be an old double-decker, converted to open-top, or possibly one "accidentally" converted by hitting a low bridge! The use of tree loppers has almost died out – probably too expensive in labour terms – so modern double-deck buses are often fitted with a vertical fender rail to protect the front window.

London Transport was also responsible for the London Underground, and their extensive service fleet included vehicles to cater for their needs. This included some old STL type buses that had been converted to incident control/breakdown tender units. These were later replaced by purpose-built vehicles, but these were constructed unusually on Leyland PD3A bus chassis, a type that did not feature in the bus fleet!

Some of these conversions were to have remarkably long lives, and so many pre-war and early post-war vehicles have survived into the preservation era, while contemporary buses from the same fleets have not. A few companies even had the foresight to put aside such vehicles for posterity long before the days of bus rallies or museums to display and house them. Portsmouth Corporation were a prime example, retaining towing lorries and a tower wagon from the 1930s.

Since privatisation, such practices of vehicle conversion have died out for a variety of reasons. Expensive, in-house workshops have largely been closed. Construction and Use regulations have been tightened up. Emissions zone restrictions may limit the use of older, less clean engines in city centres. Furthermore, the modern low-floor, rear-engine buses are probably less suited to such conversions. Companies will use the services of specialist commercial bus and truck rescue services rather than retaining their own towing vehicles.

There were also a varied selection of conventional lorries and vans used by bus companies for various purposes, but these have been generally excluded, both for space reasons and because they are of perhaps less interest than the other types above.

This book looks at a variety of service vehicles from around the country over the last fifty years, including many examples that have survived into preservation. Those buses that were converted to towing lorries, tower wagons etc. will normally have been preserved in these forms, as have the purpose-built service vehicles and ex-military towing vehicles.

The pictures have been selected to show a wide variety of the more interesting vehicle types, conversions and liveries that have appeared during this period.

All photographs are by the author.

A lot of these photographs were taken in the 1970s and 1980s when attitudes were different. Many garages had open access and you could often walk round them unchallenged. If you were, an "Is it ok to take a few pictures around the yard?" would usually be answered in the affirmative. But then came terrorism and Health & Safety legislation and in came security fencing and CCTV cameras. Photographers motives began to be viewed with suspicion. Some companies (example, South Yorkshire PTE) even tried to ban photography in their bus stations for a time.

Added to this, many town centre bus garages have been sold off for redevelopment as offices, shopping malls or housing and replaced by secure sites on industrial estates. Many bus stations have been rebuilt so that passengers do not need to cross (and are therefore banned from) the areas where vehicles are moving, so creating new challenges for photographers.

So, remember that bus garages are private property and should not be accessed without prior permission. Luckily there are now far more bus rallies, running days and Open Days where there are legitimate opportunities for photographers.

Bus conversion service vehicles – information, publicity, promotional etc

GBE 846 was a 1950 Bristol K5G, originally Lincolnshire 2136. On withdrawal it passed to Eastern National who fitted it out as a publicity vehicle and fitted it with a full front and Lodekka-style grille. The upper deck was fitted out as a cinema to show films of holiday tours. By 1976 when I photographed it at the Southend Bus Rally it was owned by the East Anglian branch of the HCVC. Despite this, by 1999 it was no longer listed as being preserved.

Obviously not going anywhere, this Lincolnshire Bristol SC was parked in Grantham bus station when seen in July 1978. This may have been used either as an information office or as a staff canteen.

Rather more mobile though was 1957 Bristol SC OFW 801. This had become what was described as a 'mobile office' and was painted in National Express white livery. Taken at Uxbridge Rally June 1978.

The SC's successor may have been this Lincolnshire Bristol RELH6G (WVL 515) which has been substantially modified for its new role as a travel office. It was noted at an Open Day event at the Lincolnshire Road Transport Museum in May 1982. The striped awning is a nice touch!

One of London Country Bus Service's first Leyland Nationals, 1972-built LN7 had a short life as a bus as it became 'InfoMotion' an information bus. It was at a vehicle rally in Enfield when seen here in May 1980.

Exeter Corporation sold out to NBC neighbours Devon General in April 1970. A batch of Leyland Panthers with Marshall bodywork on order were delivered to Devon General. One of these later became a publicity unit as seen here at the Exeter garage in May 1981. TDV 217J has since been preserved by the West Country Historical Omnibus & Transport Trust.

Crosville were unusual among National Bus Companies in buying 100 Seddon RUs. They took EPG701–50 (KFM 701–18J, OFM 719–50K) with Seddon DP47F bodies and SMG 751–800 (KFM 751–78J, OFM 779–800K) with B45D bodies in 1971–2. SMG758 (KFM 759J) became information bus G759 and was seen at the National Trolleybus Museum at Sandtoft in 1982.

The livery on this Oxford AEC Renown 339 TJO is certainly eye-catching! It had been adapted as an exhibition bus and was entered in Showbus at Woburn in 1982.

This former Sheffield Leyland Atlantean with Park Royal bodywork became South Yorkshire PTE's 'Travelling Promotion and Information Bus'. It was performing this role at the Open Day held at London Transport's Chiswick Works on 3 July 1983.

Bristol Omnibus 1255 (DAE 509K), a 1971 Bristol RELL, was converted to an information bus and was sporting National Express livery when seen here at the 1985 Sandwell Rally at West Bromwich.

Eastern Counties acquired this dual-door Bristol LH No. X82 (REL 743H) from Hants & Dorset to become a publicity bus. Hants & Dorset had latterly used it as a towing vehicle (see p. 44) Here it is seen at the East of England Showground at Peterborough surrounded by an impressive display of notice boards to attract the punters. Taken in August 1983.

By June 1985 REL 743H was lettered for Ambassador Travel, a subsidiary company of Eastern Counties.

Similar Hants & Dorset Bristol LH REL 745H became an information bus for the home fleet and passed to Hampshire Bus on division of the fleet. It was promoting the company's services at the rally held at Netley near Southampton on 13 July 1986.

The Volvo Ailsa B55.10 with Van Hool McArdle bodywork was a combination unique in Britain to South Yorkshire PTE. Built in 1977, by 1986 SHL 930S had been adapted as this 'Showbus' exhibition bus. It was present at the Sandtoft Gathering in July of that year. It was probably the successor to the ex. Sheffield Atlantean seen on page 7.

Clearly lettered to show its purpose as an information bus, Hyndburn Transport OTF 358K was a 1972 Bristol RESL6L with East Lancs bodywork. It was parked in the centre of Accrington in July 1987. Hyndburn's fleet livery was red and blue.

It may not be immediately obvious with that heavily modified front panel, but there is an Alexander body on this Daimler Fleetline chassis. Originally Yorkshire Woollen District 693 it had become an information bus for United Counties when taken in 1987.

Leicester were an early advocate of the Metro-Scania single-decker and the Scania Metropolitan double-deck version. Former bus 225 became this attractive information bus seen here at a rally held there in Abbey Park during 1988. ARY 225K has since been preserved and restored to bus condition by the Leicester Transport Heritage Trust.

The ex-Hants & Dorset dual-door Bristol LH we saw earlier (see p. 11) continued to serve as an information bus as it passed from Hampshire Bus to Solent Blue Line. Here it is parked in the centre of Southampton in the area where many of their services departed from in June 1988. Hants & Dorset used to have a proper bus station at West Marlands, opposite the city hall, but this was closed to be sold off and redeveloped as the Marlands Shopping Mall which opened in September 1991, leaving only on-street departure points.

At the Trans-Lancs Rally, Heaton Park, Manchester, in September 1989, Greater Manchester PTE had XJA 534L a standard Park Royal-bodied Leyland Atlantean which had become a publicity vehicle.

Heading along the seafront at Great Yarmouth in 1989 is the local corporation's publicity bus, an AEC Swift/Willowbrook of 1972. As the lettering implies, Great Yarmouth had a blue livery.

West Midlands PTE 1976 Leyland National KOM 792P became an information bus. It was seen here at the Tyseley Railway Centre in September 1988.

Another Leyland National and another striped awning. This one was doing the honours for Trent at Woburn in September 1989. OCN 744M had started out in Northern General's Venture subsidiary fleet as No. 4498 in 1973.

This Leyland National has been adapted for Thamesway. The centre door now features a (rather steep) disability ramp – this was before the days of kneeling buses. UCO 46L is one of the large fleet of Leyland Nationals that were bought by Plymouth Corporation from 1972–4 and sold off a few years later. This one came to Eastern National as a mobility equipped bus No. 2200 in turn passing on to Thamesway. Taken at Showbus, Duxford, 1993.

Provincial bought this Alexander-bodied Leyland Atlantean from Waddon, Caerphilly in 1988 which became an information bus. WTN 658H was originally Newcastle No. 658. It was taken at the Southsea Rally in May 1992.

The message is clear and to the point on Yorkshire Traction L99, a Bristol LH from the Lincolnshire fleet. Taken at Sandtoft, July 1996.

London Transport RCL2221 was first adapted as a cinema bus when it was bought back from London Country (see p. 63). It later became an information bus as seen here in April 1999, just round the corner from Liverpool Street station.

Rather modest branding compared to some we have seen adorns this former First Potteries Bristol RESL. It was working for Greater Manchester North at the time and was seen at Wythall Bus Museum in August 1999.

Its days as an 'Exhibus' over, this former Manchester Leyland Atlantean is now with the SELNEC Preservation Society. It was Manchester 1066 with Park Royal bodywork and was seen at Heaton Park, Manchester in September 1999.

Leeds-based coach company Wallace Arnold had this former Southdown Leyland PD3 BUF 425C, which was seen in their home city during 1994.

A later vehicle used by Wallace Arnold as a hospitality coach was this Volvo Ailsa/Alexander which has been given a personalised registration. It was being used as a rally control vehicle at Showbus, Duxford, in 1997. Later it would receive the company's cream livery as carried by the earlier PD3.

This Isle of Man National Leyland National was being used by the Manx Tourist authorities to promote the island's railway attractions in 1993 and has been given this special registration for the duration. It was touting for customers at the 1992 Great Dorset Steam Fair.

The West Midlands Passenger Transport Executive was formed in 1969, merging the fleets of Birmingham, Walsall, West Bromwich and Wolverhampton. Coventry would be added in 1974. WMPTE JOJ 555 was a 1951 Guy Arab IV with typical Metro-Cammell bodywork from the Birmingham fleet that had been adapted as a Travelcard sales bus. It was promoting these in Coventry in June 1974.

East Kent AEC Regent V MFN 946F became a Freedom Ticket sales bus and was photographed in Dover during July 1976. This has been preserved by Stagecoach, who acquired the East Kent fleet on privatisation, and is now part of their heritage fleet, back in pre-NBC maroon and cream. Bodywork is by Park Royal.

Nottingham received their first batch of Leyland Nationals in 1973. Nine years later and No. 728 had become an Easy Rider travel card sales bus, parked up in the City Hall square.

As we have seen, Leyland Nationals seem to have been a popular choice to turn into information offices or sales buses – mind you almost every NBC company had plenty of them. Brighton & Hove adapted this one as a travel shop, pictured on Brighton sea front in May 1986. NHE 406M had started out as Yorkshire Traction 406.

This Maidstone & District Bristol VR KKE 739N has been adapted as a mobile billboard, apparently available for hire. On this occasion it was promoting the company's own fare schemes and was passing through Maidstone in March 1992.

Bus conversion service vehicles – recovery/towing lorries

Portsmouth Corporation converted this 1931 Crossley Condor double-decker to a recovery vehicle in 1950. When withdrawal came the company put it aside for preservation long before there was the facility to display it. It is the only known example of a Crossley Condor to survive and features Crossley's own 9.12-litre diesel engine. On this occasion it had visited the Cobham Gathering at Brooklands in 1996.

This 1935 Birmingham Daimler COG5 was converted to a towing lorry. It is now in the care of BaMMOT at Wythall. In 1990 it travelled all the way to the Southsea Rally.

Southdown converted a batch of these 1938 Leyland Titan TD5 buses to recovery vehicles and at least four survive in preservation. 0184 (EUF 184) was taken in April 2007, and this is owned by the Southdown Omnibus Trust, normally kept at Amberley Museum.

BOW 162 is a 1938 Bristol L5G originally with a Beadle bus body as Hants & Dorset TS662. It became towing vehicle 9081. When photographed at a rally at Didcot in June 1986, it was in the care of Bournemouth Transport Museum who had painted it in the traditional Bournemouth Corporation yellow livery, but it has since changed hands to the West of England Transport Collection.

Alexander 205, a 1939 Leyland Tiger TS8. Seen at the Scottish Vintage Bus Museum, Lathalmond, where it is part of their extensive collection.

Preserved United 61 is a 1940 Bristol K5G/ECW, originally bus BDO23 before being cut down to a towing vehicle in 1956 and fitted with this stylish full front. This was taken at York, September 1983.

A venerable vehicle still in service with Bournemouth in January 1972 was FRU 180. This was a survivor from a batch of wartime Guy Arab II buses supplied in 1943 with Park Royal 'utility' bodywork. It had been converted as a towing lorry and was seen at the garage. These Guys had been the first diesel-powered buses in the fleet – all pre-war buses had petrol engines.

Seen parked outside Hove garage in August 1973 Southdown/BHD towing lorry W4 was a 1948 Bristol K5G originally registered EAP 4 and had been Brighton, Hove & District fleet number 6396. This later passed into preservation, but I believe subsequently got burnt out in an arson attack.

Ribble made a neat job of converting this 1950 Burlingham-bodied Leyland PS2/3 to become towing vehicle BD1 in 1965. This appeared at a rally held in Battersea Park, London, on 5 May 1986. Alongside is former Doncaster 122 a 1951 Roe-bodied AEC Regent III.

Seen inside the Preston Corporation garage in May 1976, W74 (CRN 79) was a 1949 Leyland PS1/1 with East Lancs B34R body which had been adapted for towing. This and similar CRN 80 both survive in preservation.

This Yorkshire Traction towing vehicle had come all the way down to London's Victoria Coach Station, presumably to collect a failed coach. This was a 1952 Leyland Royal Tiger PSU1/15 with Leyland's own coach bodywork (originally C41C). It had started out as Southdown 1639 (LUF 639) reaching Yorkshire Traction via Mexborough & Swinton who converted it.

In the mid-1960s, London Transport modernised many of the RF class AEC Regal IVs used on Green Line work. A broad waistband and twin headlights were the main external features. RF79 was one of these, passing to London Country Bus Services in 1970 where it was later adapted as a towing vehicle. It is seen at a rally at Thorpe Park in September 1980, in 'as acquired' condition having been bought for preservation.

In the yard of Tappins, Wallingford, in May 1976 was their towing vehicle. The chassis of this was a rare Maudslay Marathon, the body has been cut down from a Plaxton thirty-nine-seat bus body.

Preserved West Yorkshire 4044 was cut down in 1972 from a 1953-built KSW6G double-decker. It makes an interesting sight in National Bus green – West Yorkshire buses were Tilling red and then in turn National Bus red. Gateshead Metrocentre Rally, 1994.

South Notts, the independent company whose main route ran between Loughborough and Nottingham created this towing vehicle from 1953 Leyland-bodied PD2 No. 53 (ORR 810). It was seen at their garage at Gotham in June 1978. South Notts would eventually be acquired by Nottingham City Transport.

This East Yorkshire towing vehicle had travelled to London to collect a failed coach and was parked up in the coach park at Battersea on 5 May 1980. This was a 1952 Leyland PD2/12 originally No. 574, registered MKH 83 and with a full-fronted Roe body. This did not survive into preservation but MKH 84 does survive with original Roe bus body.

Midland Red converted eleven of their home-made D7 double-deck buses to towing vehicles in 1972. The style varied according to which body workshop did the work. One of these vehicles is seen assisting a failed D9 at Cannock in November 1975. Although the identity is unclear as it is running on trade plates, this is probably the former 4739 (739 BHA) which was based at Cannock. An S14 style of grille has been fitted.

A preserved former Midland Red D7 towing lorry (originally 4767, 767 BHA) prepares to tow Wolverhampton trolleybus DUK 833 from a very wet and muddy Sandwell Rally at West Bromwich on 8 May 1983.

The same vehicle. After changing hands in 1999, this was fully restored, being completed in April 2018. It is now resident at the Aldridge Transport Museum near Walsall where it was seen later that year. It has been repainted in traditional Midland Red livery although they always operated in yellow. At least five of the former Midland Red D7 recovery vehicles are listed as preserved.

Western Scottish MW7022; a cut-down Bristol Lodekka running on trade plates at Glasgow in February 1976.

A rather drastic conversion was made to Eastern Counties Bristol FS LFS47 when it became towing vehicle X55. Was that caged area above the cab intended for use by tree lopping personnel? It was at Ipswich in August 1985.

East Kent's first batch of AEC Regent V buses came in 1959 with full-front Park Royal bodywork – the only batch so fitted. One of these PFN 865 was converted to a towing vehicle and is seen here with a somewhat battered front at the Maidstone & District garage in Maidstone, July 1980.

The same vehicle as it is now – fully restored and painted in traditional East Kent livery. Seen at Newbury Showground in July 2012.

Seen at the RM60 event at Finsbury Park in 2014. Preserved London Transport RM66 is an interesting 'might-have-been'. Built in 1959 and withdrawn in 1987, it was then converted to a towing/engineering support bus by Lamming of Coulsdon. However, it was deemed too light for serious towing and after two owners, passed into preservation in 1996. Since 2010 it has been based at the Swansea Bus Museum. London Transport did convert one Routemaster to single deck, RM 1368, but not as a towing vehicle (see p. 58).

Midland Red North 2225 (SBF 233) was a 1962 Leyland PD2/28 that had been acquired with the fleet of Harper Brothers, Heath Hayes. It originally carried a Northern Counties body. Converted as a towing vehicle it was photographed at Wellington garage in May 1983. This is now listed as being preserved.

Lewingtons of Cranham, Essex, had an assorted fleet of pre-owned vehicles in the 1970s. In use as a towing vehicle was this Leyland PD2 which had come from Western Scottish.

Those well-rounded corners to the side windows are the most evident clue that this Leyland towing vehicle in the fleet of Grahams of Paisley started out as one of the full-fronted Burlingham-bodied PD3s in the Ribble fleet. It was in fact Ribble 1546 (KCK 907). Taken in May 1984.

This Portsmouth Leyland PD2 was converted to a towing lorry and was seen here towing preserved trolleybus 201 away from Southsea Common at the end of the 1978 Southsea Rally.

Preston 100 was a 1961 Leyland PD3/4 converted to a towing lorry and shortened. Originally it was bus 16, registered PRN 908 and had a Metro-Cammell H39/31F body. Training bus 99 (PRN 909), seen behind it, was the next in sequence.

South Yorkshire PTE M58 was a 1948 Leyland PD2/1 towing vehicle, originally Doncaster 96 (EDT 705). This veteran was still in use in its hometown in June 1980. Note how the body has been cut behind the rear wheels, removing the stairs. This did not survive but similar Roe-bodied bus EDT 703 does.

Another towing vehicle from the South Yorkshire PTE, which unlike M58 still survives, is M10. This is a Roe-bodied Leyland PD3, but this time ex-Sheffield and with a concealed radiator. This has regained its original registration, having been OWJ 357A for a while. To its right is a former Rotherham AEC Matador (see p. 68). Both were at the 2016 Sandtoft Gathering.

Another preserved South Yorkshire PTE vehicle, M3 is a 1962 Leyland PD3/4 converted from a Doncaster Corporation bus with Roe bodywork. This carries the later livery style. The original registration was 475 HDT. Similar M4 (OWJ 354A ex-476 HDT) is also preserved. Seen at the 1999 Trans-Lancs Rally.

GCM 147E, a 1967 Leyland PD2/37 with Massey bodywork, was originally Birkenhead Corporation No. 147, later working for Merseyside PTE. This was also at the 1999 Trans-Lancs Rally.

Coventry 105 (formerly 290) one of the city's many Daimler CVG6/Metro-Cammell buses was converted for towing. Here it is at the former Sandy Lane Garage at an event in May 2012 to mark the centenary of the former Coventry Corporation Transport.

South Wales 10 (TCY 102) was an AEC Regent V, adapted for towing and seen at Swansea in January 1976. This was not a cut-down double-decker, but a double-deck chassis fitted with a Roe single-deck body. South Wales had two of these 1959 buses (TCY 101–2) and 1963 built (279–84 DWN) – they were bought for a route in Llanelly with restricted headroom.

Very little modification seems to have been made to adapt this former Red & White Bristol MW bus for towing work. It was working for National Welsh in Bridgend during May 1980.

On the other hand, this former 1961 Bristol MW coach 2111 (404 LHT) of Bristol Omnibus has been substantially rebuilt for its new role. Photographed at home at Marlborough Street garage in Bristol, August 1978. This was one of three similar conversions – the others were former 2113/4.

Crosville were another company like Bristol who converted former Bristol MW coaches as towing vehicles. This is G386 (302 PFM), formerly SMG386 of 1960, at Chester garage in September 1979.

The fleet of North Western Road Car was split up four ways under the National Bus Company in 1972. Crosville took the vehicles and garages at Macclesfield and Northwich bringing many unfamiliar vehicle types into the fleet. Among these was Alexander-bodied Leyland Leopard VDB 961 of 1963. This later became towing vehicle L317, allocated to Warrington where it was seen in May 1981.

A Clydeside Scottish Leyland Leopard towing vehicle in Glasgow bus station during September 1986. W4 was formerly Western Scottish L2041 (CAG 456C).

Glasgow, May 1987, and Clydeside Scottish MW2, a 1965 Leopard Leopard PSU3/3R with Alexander bodywork is towing failed ex-London Routemaster RM303. The Leopard had come from Western Scottish where it was originally bus L2035 (CAG 450C).

Midland Red converted some of their 1966 Plaxton-bodied Leyland Leopard PSU4/4R coaches to towing vehicles between 1997 and 1980. Former coach 5836 (GHA 336D) passed to Midland Red North when the fleet was split up, and is here at Cannock garage in June 1984, running on trade plates.

Another of this batch passed to Midland Red South and was based at Nuneaton. It was entered in the 1986 Showbus Rally at Woburn. A similar vehicle was based at Banbury.

Hants & Dorset 1969 Bristol LH 1522 (REL 743H) became towing bus 9079. It was seen outside Southampton garage in June 1979. Note that a towing bar has also been fitted at the front. This bus was later bought by Eastern Counties and converted to an information bus (see p. 10).

Yorkshire Traction L10 (YHE 237J) a 1971 Leyland Leopard PSU4B/4R with Alexander bodywork. The way this has been converted looks like half of two separate vehicles, a lorry and bus, have been joined together. Taken at Showbus, Duxford in 1999.

National Welsh E1080, a 1971 Leyland Leopard PSU4A/2R/Willowbrook ex-Western Welsh 2334 at Bridgend in May 1988.

West Midlands Leyland Leopard towing lorry 112 tows a former Walsall trolleybus out of Dartmouth Park, West Bromwich, at the 1985 Sandwell Rally.

Yorkshire Traction L7 has received a less drastic conversion than fellow Leyland Leopard L10 we saw earlier. This was emerging from Doncaster's North bus station in June 1991.

Two generations of Scottish recovery vehicles at Lathalmond. On the left is AMS 513K a 1972 Leyland Leopard originally Alexander Midland bus MPE113. On the right is WG 5245 is a 1935 Leyland Beaver TSC9, which was fitted with a towing lorry body as a replica of Alexander (Midland) 158. In fact, it was originally West Monmouthshire 13, registered AAX 27. This is currently (2018) listed by the PSV Circle as being a chassis only with the AAX 27 registration, and no longer at Lathalmond.

Kelvin Scottish was formed in June 1985 from parts of Central Scottish and Midland Scottish. From the former came this recovery vehicle converted from a 1973 Leyland Leopard with the customary Alexander bodywork. Taken at Glasgow in September 1991.

Wilts & Dorset 9087, a 1974 Bristol LH ex-Hants & Dorset 3528 converted for towing. Note the cutaway rear panels where the towing gear is installed. On tow through Poole in September 1987 is former London Transport Daimler Fleetline DMS2045 (OUC 45R) now 1907 in the W&D fleet.

Badgerline KHU 823P, a Bristol LH recovery vehicle at Bristol in 2002. Presumably these succeeded the Bristol MWs converted earlier.

Now preserved, Ulsterbus 1281 is one of a batch of Leyland Tigers dating from 1989 with Alexander (Belfast) bodies that the company converted for towing. This was an entrant at Showbus in 2017.

Bus conversion service vehicles - tower wagons

Portsmouth converted Leyland 1933 TD2 RV 3411 as a tower wagon for their trolleybus system in 1953. It was subsequently retained for preservation along with similar TD2 RV 3412 – converted for towing. Portsmouth's preserved heritage fleet is now in the care of Portsmouth Museums and RV 3411 is seen on display at the Hampshire Museums Milestones Museum in Basingstoke.

VH 6217 is a 1934 AEC Regent ex-Huddersfield that passed to Bournemouth in 1944. They converted it to a tower wagon to service their trolleybus wiring. This was an entrant at the 1975 Southsea Rally and was then part of the Bournemouth Heritage Transport Collection. In the current 2018 PSV Circle listing of preserved buses it now has an owner in Scotland.

Preserved Sheffield tower wagon CWJ 410 is a 1937 Weymann-bodied AEC Regent 1, originally bus A310 before conversion to serve the city's tram network (which lasted until 1960). It is preserved by the Tramway Museum Society at Crich, where it was seen in 1983.

Nottingham 802 (FTO 614), a 1939 AEC Regent 1 tower wagon, is preserved at the Sandtoft Trolleybus Museum. Here it was seen in 1986 posed with other preserved Nottingham vehicles; 161 (OTV 161) 1952 AEC Regent V/Park Royal and 578 (KTV 578) 1951 BUT 9641T/Brush trolleybus.

Seen at the East Anglia Transport Museum, Carlton Colville, in 1980 among other vehicles awaiting their turn of restoration, was former Eastern Counties X39 (ENG 707) a 1942 Bristol L5G converted to a tower wagon.

Preserved Bolton CWH 717 is a 1948 Leyland PD2/4 converted to a tower wagon in the 1960s. It originally carried a Leyland H30/26R body as fleet No. 364. The tower fitted to it came from an earlier horse-drawn inspection platform. CWH 717 is now with the Museum of Transport, Manchester, and was on display at the Trans-Lancs Rally at Manchester's Heaton Park in 1981.

Bus conversion service vehicles – tree loppers

London Transport 971J is the only surviving front-entrance STL and this was due to its conversion for tree pruning in 1953. Built in 1936 with Weymann bodywork for the country area, these buses had a central staircase but no doors. In service they were cold in winter and suffered from windswept litter being scooped into the body. The STL was replaced by a purpose-built Ford Thames Trader lorry registered 969 ELR in 1963. 971J was pictured at Kingscote station on the Bluebell Railway.

Dating from 1940 Southern Vectis Bristol K5G No. 703 (DDL 50) was converted to open-top in 1959. However, seen here in September 1973 it has been demoted from the operational fleet to serve as a tree lopper in NBC green and was parked up in Ryde garage yard. It lasted until 1979 in this role and was then sold for preservation and restoration to original condition.

Stevensons, Uttoxeter, PCW 945 was a 1964 Leyland PD2A/27 with Northern Counties bodywork that had come from the Burnley & Pendle fleet. Converted for tree-lopping it was at the Uttoxeter garage in June 1983.

Trent A28 (518 JRA) a 1959 Bristol LDG6 tree lopper was originally Midland General bus 652. This was at Derby garage in May 1981.

Luton & District Bristol 1021 FS6G KBD 715D. Note the trailer towed behind to store the cuttings. Seen at Luton in 1992.

The crew of Alder Valley South TL61 had obviously been hard at work to judge by the amount of foliage accumulated on the upper deck. They were taking a break in Guildford bus station when this was recorded in September 1990. The Bristol VR had originated with Thames Valley.

When London Country Bus Services started to win London routes on tendering, they bought several second-hand Leyland Atlanteans including what became AN306-36 from Strathclyde. AN330 was one of those that passed to London Country South West when the fleet was split up and they renamed themselves London & Country. This bus became a tree lopper and is at Addlestone garage in April 1991.

Thamesdown (Swindon) bought thirty-five Fleetlines with ECW bodies between 1976 and 1980. OHR 183R dated from 1977 and became tree lopper 383.

Many bus companies do not bother with tree pruning nowadays, fitting tree deflectors to their double-deckers instead. So it's interesting to see a modern view of a Stagecoach former Southdown VR adapted for such use. This was at the Southdown 100 Years Rally at Southsea in 2015.

Bus conversion service vehicles – miscellaneous

Blackpool 1937 Leyland Tiger TS7 FV 9044 became an engineering works bus and lasted long enough to reach the preservation era. Like most Blackpool buses of this period it has full-fronted bodywork by local manufacturer Burlingham. Now preserved in Sussex it is seen at the 2008 Alton Rally. Similar FV 9043 was converted to a tower wagon but has not survived.

Coventry RWK 167, a 1955 Daimler CVG6 with Metro-Cammell body, had become mobile workshop 010 by June 1974 when I photographed it in the bus station. The livery can best be described as a 'bitsa!' From 1 April 1974 Coventry Corporation passed into the West Midlands PTE.

West Midlands 414 (291 RW), a 1961 Daimler CVG6/Metro-Cammell ex-Coventry, was still in use as a works bus/tree lopper when located in the bus station in May 1980.

Blackpool 257 had become an anonymous works bus in yellow when photographed among typical Blackpool surroundings in 1989. It was a typical Leyland PD3 with Metro-Cammell body – Blackpool standard fare through the 1960s, although until 1964 full-fronts were specified.

London Transport RM1368 lost its upper deck in an arson attack on 31 December 1973. It was rebuilt in this single-deck form and used as an experimental vehicle at Chiswick Works, replacing RM8 which then went into normal service. It was an exhibit at a rally at Syon Park on 17 September 1978. This was the home of the London Transport Museum at the time, following the closure of the Museum of British Transport at Clapham and before the present site at Covent Garden became available. RM1368 has since been privately preserved.

Chesterfield bought this 1953 Leyland Royal Tiger PSU1/13 fitted with Burlingham bodywork from Bournemouth and equipped it as a mobile canteen. It was photographed in July 1976 alongside 81 (SRB 81F), a 1967 Leyland Panther with East Lancs bodywork built by their subsidiary company Neepsend.

London Country substantially rebuilt former LT RLH44 to become a uniform issue vehicle, numbered 581J. It was later preserved, and its unusual appearance can be appreciated here in this view at the 1987 Southsea Rally

London Transport's Chiswick Works and Aldenham bus overhaul works were split off as LRT Bus Engineering Ltd (later BEL Holdings) as LT was split up for privatisation. Staff buses were employed to bring in some of the workers. Preserved RCL2254 displays a livery used by BEL on some of these buses. This was seen at Brooklands.

Birmingham converted 1935 Daimler COG5 679 (AOG 679) with a new body by Riverlee of Tyseley in 1947 to become a bank van, transporting the takings from bus garages to the bank and tickets to the garages. It lasted in this role until 1967 when it passed directly into preservation. In preservation it was often then used as a towing vehicle for preserved trolleybuses. This vehicle is now based at the Aston Manor Road Transport Museum at Aldridge where it is seen in 2018 awaiting restoration.

A line-up of former London Transport service vehicles at Brooklands in 2017. Flanking the AEC Militant recovery lorry, now in National Rescue colours, are two of the breakdown tenders that were converted in 1950 from 1933 AEC Regent buses of the STL class with new Chalmers of Redhill van bodies. JJ 4379 (ex-STL162) became 832J and AGX 520 (ex-STL169) became 738J.

A nearside of 738J showing the sliding door bodywork. Four of these vehicles remained in use until at least 1970 and all four have since passed into preservation. 738J is lettered as being based at Cricklewood garage. Also preserved are 739J (AGX 517) and 830J (AXM 649).

From 1978 onwards, the National Bus Company undertook a programme of local traffic surveys as part of the Market Analysis Project [MAP]. Taken at Wakefield in June 1980 this Leyland Atlantean was being used in this role by West Riding/Yorkshire. 9322 PT had been new in 1962 as Sunderland District 322, then passing to Northern General as 3170. At this time, it was actually owned by Lincolnshire.

One of Southdown's many 'Queen Mary' Leyland PD3 buses with Northern Counties full-front bodies, 292 was adapted as a passenger survey bus, as seen here in Brighton in September 1986.

National Express were using this former West Yorkshire PTE Leyland Atlantean/Roe as a check-in and waiting room for passengers awaiting Rapide services to Birmingham at London's Victoria Coach Station in February 1989.

London Transport bought back the Routemasters that had passed to the NBC with the formation of London Country. RCL2221, originally a Green Line coach, was converted to a cinema bus in 1979 for the 150 Years of London Buses events. At that time, it was painted in 'Shillibeer' horse bus livery, but by 1981 it had been repainted red. It was seen here at the rally held at Ensign Bus's Purfleet premises in July 1981. It later became an information bus (see p. 17).

London Transport 1970 AEC Swift SMD91 was adapted as a video training bus. It featured at the Open Day held at Chiswick Works on 3 July 1983. By 1990 it had been further adapted as a mobile classroom and numbered STB91. It is now preserved by the Pump House Steam & Transport Trust at Walthamstow.

Another London Transport AEC Swift, SMS753 (JGF 753K) became a mobile shop and information bus for the London Transport Museum. It was on duty at a rally in Southampton on 7 May 1979 to celebrate the centenary of Southampton Transport.

Former Leyland National LS334 was converted to become a London Transport Museum sales bus. It was used at Covent Garden as a temporary replacement for the museum shop while the museum was closed for a refurbishment. Taken in May 1993.

A more recent sales bus was this former Ipswich Optare Excel used during the 'Year of the Bus' events in 2014. This was it within the iconic surrounds of Stockwell garage during the Open Day of 25 June 2014.

In the early 1950s, Barton rebuilt, rebodied and reregistered several old Leyland chassis to become their BTS1 class. NNN 968 was later further rebuilt to become a transporter vehicle for their preserved 1923 Daimler charabanc. It performed this role at the Open Day held at Leicester Corporations Abbey Park Road depot in 1974 to mark fifty years of motorbuses. This is now preserved as part of the Barton Cherished Vehicle Collection.

London Buses DMS1515 was converted to this unique vehicle known as 'Supercar'. It features the front bays of the original bus, behind which are mock ups of a section of tube stock and of the cab and front section of a Class 321 electric multiple unit in Network SouthEast livery. This was done for a television advertising campaign for Travelcards – day or weekly tickets valid on buses, the Underground and suburban rail services in the London area. This is now privately preserved by the London Bus Company.

Service vehicles bought new on bus chassis

From 1962–4 London Transport bought eight railway breakdown tenders for use with incidents on the Underground system. I recall that one of these was always parked on standby outside Baker Street station. Unusually these were built on Leyland Titan PD3A/1 bus chassis – a model not otherwise represented in the fleet. Of these 1279LD survives in preservation and is seen here at a rally at Lingfield in 1999. The bodywork was by Mann Egerton.

An additional railway breakdown tender came in 1966, 1416LD which had a slightly different style of bodywork. This also survives and is here at the 1997 North Weald Rally.

Service vehicles on lorry chassis – recovery/towing lorries

PO 3922 is a 1931 AEC Mammoth lorry. In 1940 Coventry Corporation converted it for bus recovery, which it did until retired in 1974, after which it passed into preservation.

No. 32 in the Aldershot & District fleet was an AEC Matador towing lorry allocated to the main depot at Aldershot. It was seen there on 17 November 1971 with a Dennis Loline III in tow. The rugged build and 4 x 4 wheel drive of these armed forces vehicles made them ideal for use as recovery vehicles. They were also widely used in the timber industry for hauling and loading cut trees and large numbers have made it into the preservation era, including this one.

Freshly repainted, this was Cardiff's AEC Matador towing lorry. It was attending a rally held in the city centre on 26 June 1983 and had just positioned a preserved ex-Cardiff trolleybus, just visible behind it. This has subsequently been preserved.

Rotherham Corporation had become part of the South Yorkshire PTE in April 1974 along with Doncaster and Sheffield, but this AEC towing lorry was still in full council identity at the garage in September 1982. This is also now preserved (see p. 38).

This AEC served with Birmingham and is seen appropriately at the AEC Society Rally at Newark Showground in 2018.

Neighbours Wolverhampton had this AEC Matador now registered LSV 833. This was taken at West Bromwich in 1987.

A Lancashire United AEC this time at Heaton Park, Manchester, in 1999.

Former Southdown 0826 arriving at Brighton at the end of the 1990 London–Brighton run. This example started with the RAF in 1945. It was bought by Southdown in 1949 and served with them until 1988.

At Trent's garage in Derby, a major fire destroyed buildings and several vehicles in July 1976. A few days later an AEC towing lorry brings the remains of one of destroyed vehicles out into the yard.

South Yorks PTE RS1 (DSA 987) was another AEC Matador. Photographed in August 1978, the bodywork on this and the Trent vehicle have been more substantially rebuilt than those pictured previously.

This 1945 AEC Matador was acquired by Southern Vectis in 1964 for conversion to a recovery vehicle and then remained in use until 1986. It is now preserved at the Isle of Wight Bus Museum in Ryde, where it is seen in 2018.

Passing through the heart of Edinburgh, this heavily rebuilt AEC Matador of Eastern Scottish has a failed Scottish Citylink liveried coach in tow. Taken in May 1987.

Seen having passed into preservation, London Transport 746P was one of four AEC Matador Master Breakdown Tenders still working with LT in 1971. These were 746/747/750/751P bought in 1948/9 and fitted with 5-ton cranes. All had originated with the Royal Air Force, and they served LT on trade plates. In preservation it was allocated registration 816 FUF.

This Southend AEC Matador was running on trade plates but also carried a London registration JXW 122. This was due to it having previously been with London Transport. It was at the Southend Rally, 5 June 1977. The AEC was extensively rebuilt in 1980 but was destroyed by a fire at the works in 1981.

Sporting the later style of AEC radiator grille is Alder Valley 1050 at Reading garage in May 1980.

This preserved AEC worked for Western Welsh. It was photographed at a rally in Basingstoke in 2011.

The body shop at Yorkshire Traction created a body design for this AEC with side flashes very typical of coach design up to the 1950s, and very smart it looks too. This was entered at the Great Dorset Steam Fair in 1999.

This AEC presumably served with Bristol, according to the blind display. This was taken at the Shrewsbury Steam Rally in 1997.

This Hampshire Bus ex-Hants & Dorset AEC Matador looks capable of dealing with just about anything. The bodywork is a credit to the skills of the bodyshop. 9094 was based at Basingstoke in October 1988.

The bodywork on this Southdown AEC Matador has been totally built in-house and shows many features of contemporary BET Federation styling – particularly the windscreen and peaked dome.

Not all AEC recovery vehicles were ex-Armed forces Matadors! This six-wheeled AEC Mammoth Major had apparently served with Valiant Silverline. It was at North Weald in 1990.

This massive AEC Militant recovery vehicle was one of two 1456–7MR with London Transport. They were built in 1964 for the Army and sold on to London Transport only two years later as Master Breakdown Tenders. These had 10-ton cranes. When seen at Canvey Island in 1997 this one was with Blue Triangle Buses. One of the pair is preserved at Brooklands where it is in National Rescue colours (see p. 60).

Another AEC six-wheel Militant that served with Trent. The new body for this has been assembled using many ECW body parts and windows. Now preserved, this was seen at Ruddington in 2000.

There's no question where the bodywork came from for this National Welsh AEC towing lorry – it's the back end of a Leyland National! The lorry is towing another stricken National ND1417 (KDW 363P). As this was photographed at the Leicester Forest Services on the M1 Motorway it is possible that the Leyland National was being taken back to the makers factory at Workington, Cumbria for repair. Taken in July 1985.

It wasn't all AECs! Taff Ely (Pontypridd) had this ex-military Scammell, now preserved.

A more modern Scammell that worked for Blue Triangle. Seen at the Southend Rally in 1993.

A more unusual choice of towing vehicle was this ex-Army Bedford S type used by Swindon. It was posed near the garage with an ECW bodied Daimler Fleetline on tow. Taken in April 1979.

London Buses 2372L was one of four Leyland Freighters bought from 1982–4 for major recovery work. It was at Aldenham Works when an Open Day was held there on 25 September 1983 as part of the LT fifty years celebrations.

A Leyland Freighter, by now working for London General, takes a failed Routemaster on suspended tow. This was spotted outside Victoria station on 21 October 2003. The Leyland is carrying the registration originally on RM46. The Routemasters blinds have been set (appropriately) to 'Not in Service'.

Oops! This National Travel South West Leyland Leopard has embarrassingly failed at Heathrow Airport and has had to be rescued by their Foden towing lorry. Hopefully an alternative coach was found to convey the passengers. Taken on 14 June 1984.

This Maidstone & District AEC was pictured on Brighton seafront on 21 September 1986. There was a rally to celebrate eighty-five years of Brighton buses and this was probably there to provide backup support in case any vehicles broke down.

This 1976-built Scammell Crusader six-wheeler provided heavy recovery support at Badgerline's Weston-Super-Mare depot. It was on hand at the 1985 Bristol Rally.

A Foden recovery truck operated by Cheltenham & Gloucester and seen in Gloucester bus station in June 1987. Judging by the lettering, they offered commercial recovery services as well as to their own vehicles.

This six-wheeled Atkinson worked for Eastern National before preservation. It carries a cast fleet number plate and CF garage code for Chelmsford. Taken at Canvey Island in 2012.

This former Chiltern Queens Guy was seen towing ex-Reading trolleybus 113 into the ring at the Woodcote Steam Rally in 2011.

At Manchester Piccadilly, this Bee Line DAF has come to the rescue of a failed Stevensons bus in July 1996.

One company still using their own recovery vehicle was bus operators and dealers Ensignbus of Purfleet, Essex. Their Volvo truck was towing Jersey Leyland TD2 No. 25 (6332 J originally J 6332) after it had been on display at Lakeside bus station during the 2016 Ensignbus Running Day. The Leyland's engine was undergoing restoration and was not installed at the time.

Service vehicles on lorry chassis – tower wagons

Probably the oldest surviving bus company service vehicle is this tower wagon from Leicester. Dating from 1911, this remarkable Leyland was still in use during the Second World War. It is now preserved and housed at the Abbey Pumping Station in Leicester, where it was photographed in 2012

Ransomes Sims & Jefferies were an Ipswich-based company who moved from the manufacture of steam traction engines to electric vehicles including trolleybuses in the 1920s. Ipswich Corporation replaced their trams with trolleybuses, including Ransomes vehicles, and also bought DX 3578 this battery-powered tower wagon driving motors on the front wheels, which dates from 1922. It survives in preservation at the East Anglian Transport Museum at Carlton Colville, Lowestoft, where it was noted in 2019.

A later Ipswich tower wagon was this 1948 AEC Monarch seen at the Constantine Road garage in 1985. Now also preserved, in this case at the local Ipswich Transport Museum.

London Transport needed many tower wagons for its extensive tram and trolleybus network. 89Q (DGJ 181) was one of a batch new in 1936. After the end of trolleybuses in 1962 it was sold and later the tower was removed, and the AEC Mercury used as a towing lorry. It was acquired by the London Transport Museum in 1985 and has been restored to the original format. Seen visiting the London Bus Museum at Brooklands in 2017.

Huddersfield tower wagon MVH 388 was one of a pair of AEC Mandator vehicles supplied in 1958. This was preserved by the West Yorkshire Transport Museum where it was on display in July 1990. The other vehicle MVH 387 was converted into a recovery vehicle in 1964.

Reading 332 was a 1958 AEC Mercury ex-London Transport 1076Q. Here it is at a rally in Uxbridge in June 1977 (a predecessor of Showbus). It is towing ex-London Transport trolleybus 1812, which was exhibited having been brought back to England following further service in Spain with the Santandar-Astillero fleet.

A collection of preserved tower wagons await their turn of restoration at Sandtoft in 1988. On the right is another Reading vehicle; CDP 583, a Morris Commercial. On the left is former Bradford XKW 833 a 1962 Austin. The middle vehicle is an ex-Bradford Karrier Gamecock.

Formerly with the City of Manchester was this 1947 Thornycroft Sturdy tower wagon. Manchester operated trolleybuses from 1938 until the end of 1966.

This Brighton Corporation 1935 Dennis Ace was used to maintain the overhead when trolleybuses were operated between 1939 and 1961. The Dennis was sold in 1962 and passed through two owners without being restored. Found and purchased in 1990 it was restored over two years and entered in the 1993 HCVS London–Brighton run.

This 1965 Albion of Walsall Corporation was towing a preserved Walsall trolleybus from the Sandwell Rally in nearby West Bromwich. Taken in May 1980.

Former Bradford Austin tower wagon doing what it was designed to do – maintaining the overhead wires, in this case at the National Trolleybus Museum at Sandtoft.

Blackpool did not operate trolleybuses, but had, and still has, trams. This Mercedes Unimog YFV 577Y was part of the service fleet. It is fitted with a revolving broom on the front – perhaps to sweep drifting sand from the tracks. It was designed to run on the tram tracks as well as on the road and had a tow bar to tow trams. Seen here doing some maintenance at the depot, such tower wagons were also highly useful in erecting the famous illuminations.

Service vehicles on lorry or van chassis – other uses

Arriving at the seafront at the end of the 1919 London–Brighton run, KR 1765 is a 1930 Morris Light Van. It is owned by the Southdown Omnibus Trust at Amberley Museum and has been painted to represent a typical service van used by Southdown in the 1930s.

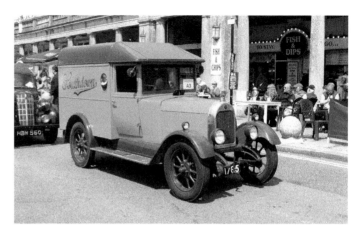

This Morris J van was preserved in the maroon and cream colours of the West Monmouthshire Omnibus Board (the Bedwellty & Mynyddislwyn UDCs), until 1970 when they changed to light blue and cream. After local government changes in 1974 the company became Islwyn Borough Transport. Taken at Barry Island in 1994.

This South Midland Bedford van is preserved in the Oxford Bus Museum.

This Land Rover was used as a towing vehicle by Midland Red and is now an exhibit at the Wythall Bus Museum.

London Transport 1282F, a 1963 Ford Thames Trader, was one of many such chassis they bought in the 1960s. This carries a box body as an auxiliary breakdown tender. It was at the Open Day held at Chiswick Works on 4 August 1984 and was retained for preservation.

This Dennis box van was seen in the colours of Trent Motor Traction. I photographed this at a rally in Leicester in 1992 but have not seen it since.

Preserved in the Museum of Transport at Manchester is this 1926 Karrier towing lorry on solid tyres. Originally a petrol tanker for Shell-Mex, it was purchased by Stockport Corporation for conversion and was in occasional use as late as 1970, hence its survival into the preservation era.

Two London Transport service vehicles in the London Bus Museum collection at Brooklands are 1096F, a 1959 Ford Thames 300E light van, and 1492B, a 1968 Bedford CAL ambulance with Lomas body, which was based at Aldenham Works. Similar ambulance 1532B, which used to be at Chiswick Works is also preserved at Brooklands.

London Transport 702B is the sole survivor of thirteen of these Bedford canteen units built in 1948 (Olympics year) for use at remote locations and special events. Using a Bedford OSS tractor unit with Scammell coupling and a trailer built by Spurlings of Hendon. The last of these remained in service until 1967. This was one of the first to go, being withdrawn and sold to Liverpool Corporation in 1959 for further use there. It passed into preservation in 1973 and is part of the London Bus Museum collection at Brooklands. At the early Cobham Open Days, this was used to provide catering for the visitors, but I suspect that modern Health and Safety legislation would not permit this now.

GXY 19 was a Maudsley Mogul Mark II tanker lorry built in 1944 for the wartime Pool Board. It was later acquired by London Transport as 1014MY, part of their service fleet. It remained in their ownership until at least 1971. It then passed into preservation and was noted at a vehicle rally held at Alexandra Palace in August 1979. I later saw it repainted out of LT livery but have not seen it since so I do not know if it still survives.

Former Southdown 0823 is this 1965 AEC Mammoth Major tanker. It was seen at Cobham Bus Museum in April 1986 marked as 'For sale'.

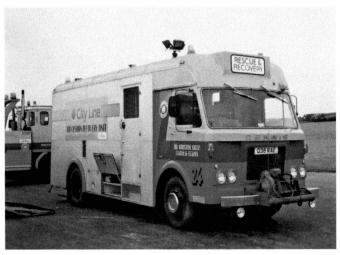

This Dennis recovery unit operated by Bristol City Line appears to have been a former fire service vehicle. It was present at the 1988 Bristol Rally.

Miscellaneous

This 1942 Fordson tractor was the last of nine built for London Transport for use in depots, shunting trams, trolleybuses and buses. 626X served at Hertford, St Albans and Edgware at various times until withdrawn in 1966. It now resides at the East Anglia transport Museum at Carlton Colville.

This Eastern Counties Lacre street broom is preserved at the Ipswich Transport Museum.

Acknowledgments and Bibliography

Booth, Colin, *Bus Ancillary Vehicles: The Municipal support fleet* (Hersham, Ian Allan, 2001)

Wright, Colin, *Trucks in Britain Vol. 4: Bus Company Service Vehicles* (Skipton, Wyvern, 1985)

PSV Circle, *Preserved Buses: (2018 edition)* (Barking, The PSV Circle, 2018)

Various fleet lists over the years published by the PSV Circle, Ian Allan, Capital Transport, LOTS etc.